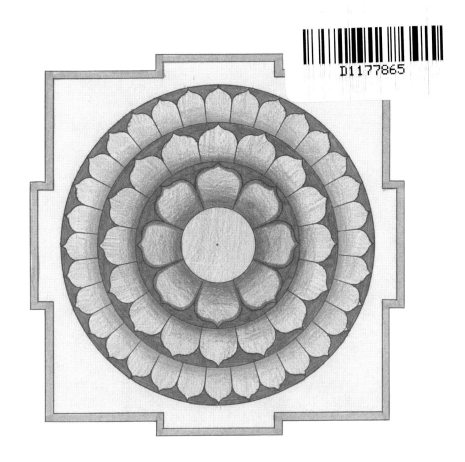

Setting the Table:

A Guide for Diversified Learner Program Development in Catholic Schools

By Crystal Brooks and Colleen McCoy-Cejka

NCEA®
National Catholic Educational Association

www.NCEA.org

ISBN: 978-1-55833-708-4
Part No.: ADM-70-1609

TABLE OF CONTENTS

Foreward by Michael J. Boyle, Ph.D.. v

Chapter 1: Where it Begins 1

Chapter 2: Special Education 101 7

Chapter 3: Assessing the Situation.. 13

Chapter 4: Blueprint for Building: A Program Framework....................... 21

Chapter 5: The Role of Leadership 31

Chapter 6: Implementation 41

Chapter 7: From A Diocesan Perspective 49

Chapter 8: In Closing 55

Appendix A 59

References 61

Acknowledgements... 63

About the Authors... 64

FOREWARD

The image of "table" is strong. The table is place for us to gather, for ideas to be shared, and where family comes together to belong and love. Our Catholic schools are tables. Some students are invited to sit at the table and others are not. Sometimes, when those with disabilities are invited to the table, it is without full participation. It is not enough to be just invited, as some small token. It is critical that all are invited, that we ensure that all have a place at the table.

Increasingly, Catholic schools are answering the call to be inclusive in serving students with disabilities and, in essence, include more students at the table. However, they often do not know where to start. Catholic schools are caught in between wanting to serve more students with disabilities but not having a clear path forward. In many respects, my work, *Ensuring a Place at the Table: Serving Students with Disabilities in Catholic Schools*, is about access and equity, about getting the door open for students with disabilities. It was my attempt to offer a framework to help guide the work of Catholic schools in creating and sustaining programs for students with disabilities.

The moment of pride for any author is when other professionals use your work as a jumping off point and develop practical applications for implementation. For me, *Setting the Table: A Guide for Diversified Learner Program Development in Catholic Schools* is that moment of pride. The authors, Crystal Brooks and Colleen McCoy-Cejka, have taken their experience in the area of supporting students with disabilities in Catholic school settings and have used the frameworks offered in *Ensuring a Place at the Table* to create actionable steps for designing and implementing programs. Their work extends my original work in a manner that is both practical and creative.

Building off of years of experience of delivering programming for diversified learners, the authors offer steps that have been used in the field and have used that experience to refine the original framework. This reference guide has many examples that help to illuminate the framework in a very practical fashion. The checklists and assessments are helpful to establish benchmarks to monitor staff progress in developing the essential knowledge, skills and dispositions to support programming for students with disabilities in Catholic schools.

Setting the Table: A Guide for Diversified Learner Program Development in Catholic Schools provides a much needed resource that has been missing in the field. For those readers that are seeking ways to increase their capacity to serve all of God's children, this resource is a place to start.

Michael J. Boyle, Ph.D., Director
Andrew M. Greeley Center for Catholic Education
School of Education
Loyola University Chicago

CHAPTER 1:
WHERE IT BEGINS

*Truly, I say to you, as you did it to one of
the least of these my brethren, you did it to me.*

MATTHEW 25:40

One evening, my son excitedly called to me from the living room, saying, "Look, mom--look at this story on the news! See, this is why every person should have someone with autism in their class--so they know the difference between a person on drugs and a person with autism! What is wrong with people?" We shook our heads while we watched the body-cam footage of a struggle between a police officer and a teen boy who was mistaken to be a threat when he was performing a self-regulating exercise in a park west of Phoenix, Arizona.

> *"On July 19, 2017, a teen boy in Buckeye, Arizona, was approached by a police officer because of behavior the officer interpreted to be drug-related. The officer grabbed and attempted to restrain the boy, as the scared teen tried to tell him he was "stimming." In the struggle, the officer and teen hit a tree and fell to the ground. The officer intended to pin down the boy and handcuff him, but the boy's caretaker arrived on the scene and tried to deescalate the situation. "He pushed me down on the grass and he just hit me on the tree, and he tackled me and then he didn't stop," Leibel later told <u>CBS News</u>. "It made me feel sad. Fourteen year-old Connor Leibel was calming himself by stimming when his life changed."*

My son, who was 13 at the time, did not realize the profundity of his statement. He was 100% correct! Every person we encounter deserves understanding. But how do we learn to interact with people who exhibit non-typical behaviors when we do not grow up with them in the same environments where we live and learn?
*(**The Be Safe Program, a training mechanism to help service providers including police interact with persons with autism, is now available. This program also helps persons with Autism Spectrum Disorder (ASD) learn to interact with police.)*
Based on my own observations as a student, teacher, and administrator for Catholic schools beginning in the late 1970s, learning, working, teaching, and praying with class-

mates or students I could identify as being non-neurotypical (that is, people who displayed atypical thought patterns or behaviors) or physically handicapped were not the norm in my classrooms and schools. While higher incidence disabilities were a bit more identifiable, especially from the mid-90s forward in my career, clear pathways of support for students who struggled academically, socially, or behaviorally were still not the norm.

Catholic schools have the opportunity to bring the virtues to life in the classroom every day. It is not enough to study the virtues. Kindness and patience, along with charity, love, and generosity, must be learned and practiced in action, not as a philosophy. Encountering and accompanying those who are physically, mentally, socially, or developmentally different from ourselves causes us to stretch the limits of our humanity. Segregating ourselves from interactive experiences limits what we learn about our world, God's creations, and our own capabilities as Christian humans. We must get out of our comfort zones if we are to do God's work. For many years I have heard the argument that students with disabilities belong in public school, where they have more resources. In some cases, this is true, but Catholic schools can do so much more than they think at the outset. We cannot abandon our call to witness and challenge ourselves to grow in practice.

That being said, coming to this realization has been a long and winding road in my life. So, when I speak to groups or individuals about the importance of inclusive practices, it's not because it all came so naturally to me. Quite the contrary.

My teaching career began in public school where the teachers in the special education department were attentive, supportive, and ever-present to help me with identified students. However, having been educated in grades 1-12 in Catholic schools, I was not familiar with the concept of special education. It was absent from my entire career as a student. I took a one-semester class in college as part of teacher preparation that included information on learning disabilities, but as far as interacting with non-neurotypical classmates or physically handicapped individuals--yikes! I was inexperienced and unprepared. My second year of teaching was in a Catholic school (as have been all my years since). It was here where I discovered my own limitations with students who were identified with a variety of challenges that impacted their learning.

My limitations were not only because of a lack of formal preparation, but also my disposition toward accommodations for students was unhealthy. I did not understand the difference between fair and equitable. I was faced with a variety of students with executive functioning issues, mild to moderate dyslexia, autism, Attention Deficit Hyperactivity Disorder (ADHD), and other learning disabilities as well as English Language Learners. I did not understand any of these learning differences, and I thought the students should just work harder to meet my expectations. As an English teacher, I realized that not all of my students loved reading and writing on as many levels as I did, so I made great efforts to teach in ways that would reach different learning styles. At least I had that in my teaching toolbox! I was a firm believer in multiple intelligences, knowing the learning styles of my audience, and trying to reach my students in ways that made sense to them.

Strangely, when it came to making accommodations for students identified with special learning needs, I was quite stubborn. I did not think it was fair to all of the other students to change the parameters of an assignment or (God forbid!) an assessment for one child, even if he or she had a particular learning issue. I was very hard on my students in that regard, and I did not give an inch. I did not like to repeat myself; I thought that was a problem of inattentive students. I did not like to have to write anything in a student's planner; it was on the board, for goodness sake, just write it down! Under no circumstance would I shorten an assessment, even a research paper. Thinking back, it is a miracle how well my students performed despite my inflexibility. They were amazing students, and if I had been just slightly more evolved as a professional (perhaps as a kinder human), I would have been able to get even that much more out of them! If I had prioritized love for the children over the love of my subject, my classroom would have been a different place. I am grateful to have had a phenomenal principal and a wonderful colleague (the resource teacher) who taught me so much and exercised great patience with me as I learned. I am grateful to those teaching colleagues who were models for how I should do things, and students who I never got to tell—or show—how amazing I thought they were.

Because my early years of teaching were in the Archdiocese of Indianapolis where resource teachers were a regular part of the landscape and accommodating students with high incidence disabilities was just part of the framework, I learned more each year. Over time, my knowledge grew, my skills increased, and relationships with my students (and their parents) began to improve. I became more intentional to learn individual student's needs and capabilities, which parents and students recognized as genuine care of the person. Once I moved beyond prioritizing academic achievement and into a whole-child development mindset, a shift in my relationships with others occurred.

Distinct and permanent change came seven years into my teaching career when my first child was born. Before the age of two, he had been diagnosed with a nonverbal learning disability (which eventually became an autism diagnosis). Once I became a parent of a child with autism, the entire world changed, especially the way I viewed the world of education.

Our first language was American Sign Language because my son did not speak until he was three and a half. He was taught to speak in sentences by speech and language pathologists in a developmental preschool in Munster, Indiana, which he attended for two years. When it came time for kindergarten, my husband and I, both Catholic school educated, had a hard choice to make. In a candid conversation with a public school principal (the principal of the public school my son would have attended, who sent her own daughter to Catholic schools), we became convinced that our son should be in a Catholic environment. Advocating for him made me a stronger advocate for all students with learning challenges—and smoothed my edges a bit.

It was through our search for outside therapies and support once we moved to Scottsdale, Arizona, that I met Crystal Brooks, the co-creator of this project. The number of people who have come into my life through this path has helped me to realize how the Holy Spirit is present in my life and work. My family has traveled a long, sometimes hard, but incredibly enlightening road in coming to this point, and we are so grateful for the journey.

My son would not be the inspiring person or the successful student he has become without his Catholic school experiences. I dare say, while always the struggling learner, he has often been the unexpected teacher to those around him as well.

Wherever you are in your professional or personal journey, Crystal and I want to provide some practical guidance for all educators interested in expanding inclusive practices in their Catholic schools and classrooms. We believe firmly in the mission of the Catholic Church when it comes to educating those who seek a Catholic education. We believe all are welcome and should be allowed a space at the table. We hope to provide practical guidance!

—*Colleen McCoy-Cejka*

The Need for a Structured Approach

In schools where the dispositions of leaders and teachers are high and the desire to enthusiastically jump in quickly without structures in place, trial and error becomes the default process. Sometimes, progress occurs despite a lack of strategic approach. However, taking time from the start and channeling enthusiasm into the creation of a plan for success is the best tactic. Keeping in mind that there most likely are already students in every school who have learning disabilities and a variety of challenges that impact their educational success, jumping in with those already in your care cannot wait. A deeper, more palpable awareness of a need to meet the needs of all students can drive the process of program development.

Consideration of acceptance of new students who have significant disabilities or that present challenges not faced previously by the school should be handled carefully if a structured plan for admissions is not yet in place. In Michael Boyle's 2018 book, *Ensuring a Place at the Table*, he advises to avoid ad hoc approaches when a family requests acceptance to a Catholic school. It is in a lack of structure that we may become inconsistent because we doubt our abilities and shut people out or jump to admit students we cannot serve appropriately. An example of this would be if the school principal decides to hire a 1:1 aide following the admission of a student with Down syndrome without the training component for the teacher and aide to learn how to provide an inclusive environment for the student. Then, when a student with ADHD is admitted, fidgets are purchased yet the teacher is not provided information for setting up a program to use them to increase attention to task. These then become toys that are played with in the classroom. Both situations are well intended efforts to provide the students the supports they will need for success but they lack the structural supports required for success. Once a structure is in place, a school can confidently work with families to determine fit, put supports in place, and approach the response strategically. Hoping for success is great, but a strategic plan is better.

The need for structure applies to a number of areas.
- The admissions process
- Identifying current students who may have exceptional needs
- The interview and hiring process

- Regular procedures teachers are trained and expected to follow as employees of a school

All of these aspects are included in the framework provided in this book. The point is that intentional formation of a formal, consistent approach to programs for exceptional learners is crucial. The more intentional each step is, the more likely each child will succeed in the school.

TABLE 1

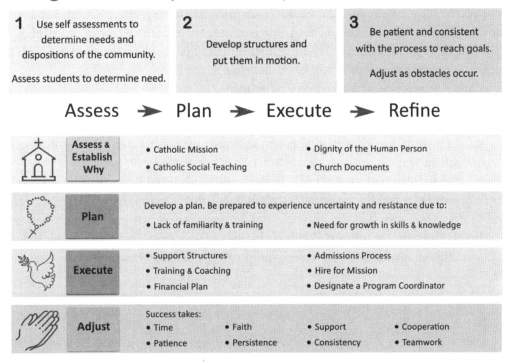

Program Development & Implementation Process

1 Use self assessments to determine needs and dispositions of the community.

Assess students to determine need.

2 Develop structures and put them in motion.

3 Be patient and consistent with the process to reach goals.

Adjust as obstacles occur.

Assess ➤ Plan ➤ Execute ➤ Refine

	Assess & Establish Why	• Catholic Mission • Catholic Social Teaching	• Dignity of the Human Person • Church Documents
	Plan	Develop a plan. Be prepared to experience uncertainty and resistance due to: • Lack of familiarity & training	• Need for growth in skills & knowledge
	Execute	• Support Structures • Training & Coaching • Financial Plan	• Admissions Process • Hire for Mission • Designate a Program Coordinator
	Adjust	Success takes: • Time • Faith • Patience • Persistence	• Support • Cooperation • Consistency • Teamwork

We Understand WHY, Now Tell us HOW!

Some time should be spent on educating your school community on the true mission of Catholic education. It is not unusual to encounter resistance on this issue. It is also quite common to learn that many Catholic educators are not familiar with Canon Law or specific teachings of the Catholic Church on this topic. Review documents with your community that address Catholic mission and persons with disabilities. Some recommendations are the United States Conference of Catholic Bishops (USCCB) Pastoral Statement on Persons with Disabilities (1978), the National Standards and Benchmarks for Effective Catholic Elementary and Secondary Schools (NSBECS), a statement from your local (arch)bishop, Catholic social teaching on the dignity of the human person, statements by the National Catholic

Partnership on Disability, Canon 795, and much more. Establish why it is part of our privilege as Catholic school educators to work toward inclusive practices. Once the *WHY* is established, the contents of this book can assist with *HOW* to make it happen.

The *HOW* will take time, patience, and persistence. This kind of change or large-scale program development will not happen overnight, in a semester, a summer training, or even one school year. Prepare yourself and your community that work this important is like hosting a banquet. Dr. Boyle imagined a table where all God's children are welcome. Where each person sits, the type of chair they sit in, what foods they eat, and the utensils they use will vary. We will now set the table to be sure everyone who is invited can share in the meal.

You know the WHY. The HOW comes next.

As we set the stage for the contents of this book, there are some presuppositions about your school community that will be made. These practices are essential when you have high expectations for students and staff. These assumptions will permit us to move into the HOW specific to inclusive practices within Catholic schools.

Basic Assumptions of the School Community:

1. Leaders and teachers are prepared to collect data and have a basic understanding of data analysis.
2. Leaders and teacher have opportunities for professional development during the school year.
3. Leadership, staff, and teacher leaders will be expected to promote a message of inclusivity for diverse learners with enthusiasm and positivity.

If you find your community is lacking in one of these areas, start there. Resources will be found throughout the book to explore and further develop these key areas.

QUESTIONS FOR REFLECTION

- Reflect on your own personal experience as a teacher in the early years of your career. Which students were the most challenging for you to reach? Why?
- When you think about what you might have done differently in the early days, what would have made the difference in your approach with your students?
- Did you have a personal conversion moment or experience which, from that moment forward, completely changed your disposition toward children with special needs? Or were you shaped earlier in life by another inspiration to be naturally inclusive?
- When thinking about your current school community, which of the basic assumptions above seems most challenging at this time?
- What excites you the most about working with your school community toward more inclusive practices?

CHAPTER 2:
SPECIAL EDUCATION 101

For by the grace given to me I tell everyone among you not to think of himself more highly than one ought to think, but to think soberly, each according to the measure of faith that God has apportioned. For as in one body we have many parts, and all the parts do not have the same function, so we, though many, are one body in Christ and individually parts of one another. Since we have gifts that differ according to the grace given to us, let us exercise them...

ROMANS 12: 3-6

"Between 1989 and 2013, the percentage of students with disabilities who were in a general education class for 80 percent or more of the school day increased from about 32 percent to nearly 62 percent." (The Atlantic, 2017.)

Some Background

Special education is the practice of providing specially designed instruction to students with disabilities as identified through a multifaceted evaluation of the individual strengths, areas for growth and academic performance of a student. Special education is mandated by the Individuals with Disabilities Education Act (IDEA) which affords all students with disabilities the right to a free and appropriate public education (FAPE) within the least restrictive environment (LRE) (History of the IDEA). All public schools receiving federal funding such as the Elementary and Secondary Education Act (ESEA) are required to implement the IDEA in service of students with diverse learning needs. These concepts are described in Table 2, as well as the categories of eligibility for receiving special education. States may add to this list of disabilities to better meet the needs of their unique populations.

Private schools, such as parochial institutions do not receive federal grant funding and are therefore not required by law to admit and educate students with special needs. But what happens when they do it anyway? As Jesus has called all to the table, Catholic schools are called to educate all children. Committed leaders and communities can be the change to provide a Catholic education to families who choose the path of academics and faith.

TABLE 2
Source: Individuals with Disabilities Education Act

Foundations of the Individuals With Disabilities Education Act

Free and appropriate public education (FAPE):

Students are guaranteed, at public expense, an education "designed to meet their unique needs and prepare them for further education, employment, and independent living."

Least restrictive environment (LRE):

Students with disabilities are to be educated, "to the maximum extent appropriate," with nondisabled peers. Special education students are not removed from regular classes unless, even with supplemental aids and services, education in regular classes cannot be achieved satisfactorily.

Individualized education program (IEP):

A document that includes, among other requirements, the child's current level of academic and behavioral performance; measurable annual goals, and a statement of the special education and supplemental aids and services that will be required to meet those goals.

Parental rights:

Parents have the right to participate in meetings relating to the evaluation of their child's needs and development of an IEP. They also have the right to challenge an evaluation or placement decision through a formal set of procedures known as due process.

Disabilities covered under the IDEA:

Autism	Multiple Disabilities
Deaf-blindness	Orthopedic Impairment
Developmental delay (category can be used from birth through age 9)	Other Health Impairment
Emotional Disturbance	Specific Learning Disability
Hearing Impairment, including deafness	Speech and Language Impairment
Intellectual Disability	Traumatic Brain Injury
	Visual Impairment, including blindness

The IDEA is a funding source for public schools; however, adequate funding has not been provided to address the variety of services students with disabilities require for academic growth. The funding comes with mandates to provide special education and related services such as speech and language therapy and/or occupational therapy without black and white guidance to implement best practice. States supplement this funding to better address educational programs at the local level. Educational leaders and teachers in public schools would likely agree that they simply want to do to what is best for the student but the law and lack of funding gets in the way.

Finance experts within Catholic schools may consider themselves fortunate that they do not have to consider this funding source! Granted, there are barriers to overcome without the funding, however it is a blessing to be able to provide an education that is specially designed to promote the student's opportunity for success without the law to get in the way. We can do what is right for the student because it is what we are called to do.

Funding and Statistics

Special education is expensive for schools to provide. The federal government spends approximately $11.9 billion on resources and supports for students with disabilities. This breaks down to $1742 of federal funds per student across the country and it is not enough. States also contribute millions of dollars, specific and individual to their funding formulas, to bridge the shortfall of IDEA funds to schools.

Private schools are entitled to a "proportionate share" of these funds to support the educational needs of children who are identified as having a disability. Public school districts are required by law to identify all exceptional learners who attend private schools within their boundaries (not where the student resides). These students are referred to as "parentally placed in private schools." Students who are suspected of having a disability or need special education services can go to the school district office where an evaluation and necessary supports can be facilitated. It is necessary for the Catholic school to have a representative available to work with the family and the public school to help coordinate. Collaboration with the family will be necessary because the school district already has so many students to support with special education services, students who are parentally placed in private schools will not be the first priority.

The "proportionate share" can be complicated for schools to compute. There is diversity in amounts and allocations per school, district, and state based upon funding formulas, however this funding remains insufficient. See Appendix A for additional information regarding the calculation of proportionate share.

In public schools across the country, 13% of students enrolled (6.7 million) are eligible for special education, based on data reported by the National Center for Education Statistics (NCES) from 2015. Among these students, 1% are parentally placed in private schools. As described in Table 2, there are thirteen categories of eligibility for special education. These categories can be further broken down as high incidence and low incidence disability categories.

Low incidence disabilities are those which include 20% of individuals with disabilities, while high incidence disabilities accounts for 80% of students with disabilities.

The common denominator for most of these high incidence disabilities is average to above average intelligence, however according to a survey by the National Center for Learning Disabilities (NCLD), 43% of those asked believed that IQ is correlated with learning disabilities (2014). By excluding students with high incidence disabilities such as Specific Learning

Disabilities, Emotional Disabilities, Speech and Language Impairments, and ADHD, we limit the potential they possess to learn and grow in a Catholic community. When considering enrollment and admissions in a Catholic school, this would exclude over 2,814,000 of school

TABLE 2.1

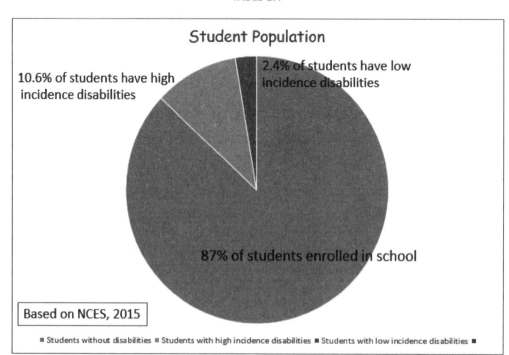

Low Incidence Disabilities	High Incidence Disabilities
Hearing Impairment	Specific Learning Disabilities (Dyslexia, Dyscalculia, Dysgraphia, Processing Deficits)
Vision Impairment	Emotional Disabilities
Deaf-blindness	Speech and Language Impairments
Autism	Developmental Delays
Multiple Disabilities	Mild Intellectual Disabilities
Orthopedic Impairments	Attention Deficit Hyperactivity Disorder (ADHD) (Other Health Impairments)
Traumatic Brain Injury	
Other Health Impairments*	
Moderate to Severe Intellectual Disabilities	

*(OHI includes: asthma, attention deficit disorder, attention deficit hyperactivity disorder, diabetes, epilepsy, cardiac conditions, hemophilia, leukemia, rheumatic fever, sickle cell anemia, and nephritis)

aged children across the country! (Per the NCLD, 2014, 42% of students found eligible for special education have a specific learning disability).

Specific Learning Disability is the most prevalent category of eligibility in our public schools, according to the NCLD (2014). For most students identified, being in the general education environment promotes better outcomes for students with learning disabilities (NCLD, 2014). When considering the statistics in our Catholic schools, there may be tens of thousands of students with disabilities already enrolled across the nation, with a large number of them diagnosed with a specific learning disability. Those are only the students who have been identified. Now consider the student you may have encountered over the years in a Catholic school who always struggled, was retained, had behavioral issues in the classroom, etc. Was he or she never diagnosed? Did he or she receive the instructional environment that would lead to successful completion of high school or college? We know WHY we need to support these students, however our resources are lacking...

Resources for Support

Why the high costs? The expense for educating students with disabilities comes from the resources required for success. Consider what is required to teach a child to read with braille, or to provide the supports required for a student in a wheelchair. Invisible disabilities such as dyslexia, speech and language impairments or ADHD also require resources and support for academic success. Next, consider the fact that most teachers working in elementary and secondary education have a general education or content specific degree that did not prepare them to meet the needs of students who learn differently or struggle with academic content. Despite the fact that the IDEA has required students to be taught in the least restrictive environment (often the general education classroom for students with high incidence disabilities), most colleges and universities are not graduating educators who can meet student needs in this setting. Specialists to work directly with the students, support teachers and families, and complete the administrative tasks of coordinating accommodations are often difficult to recruit and may have a specialized academic degree.

Space on campus will need to be allocated perhaps at the expense of a program that brings in revenue for the school. Professional development outside of what you can offer locally may be expensive, however there are Title funds that can be accessed for educators to attend conferences which can lessen the direct costs. Specialized curriculum to facilitate tiers of intervention, and/or technology may need to be purchased so that all students can access the content in the classrooms. This description is not exhaustive, but you likely get the idea. Educational leaders must focus on how to overcome these challenges!

While implementing this framework will not eliminate costs for educating students with learning differences, it will provide the opportunity to look at financial resources with an inclusive eye, considering the knowledge, skills, and dispositions that faculty, staff, and leaders will need for success.

Inclusive Practices

- Catholic social teaching includes the promotion of inclusive practices within society, thereby extending into the manner with which students with disabilities are provided a Catholic education. Inclusion promotes a sense of belonging to the school, an understanding that the school includes all students in activities, and an emphasis on differentiated instruction in the classroom (Shogren et al., 2015). When considering the inclusion of students with disabilities within the Catholic school environment, there are six factors within the seven themes of Catholic social teaching that are relevant: Solidarity, Option for the Poor and Vulnerable, Call to Family, Community and Participation, Rights and Responsibilities, and Life and Dignity of the Human Person (Mucci, 2015). Providing an inclusive setting in our Catholic schools is necessary to ensure our students graduate with an understanding of the tenets of Catholic social justice that can only be learned through direct experience. Our schools should represent the demographics evident in a student's community and future college or work setting, including a representative sample of individuals with disabilities. This framework will provide educational leaders, educators, and community stakeholders with the means to graduate student leaders, prepared to share God's message of love and acceptance.

How can schools be inclusive?

Inclusive environments of diverse learners are essential for individuals to find themselves among all of God's children. Educators and researchers have documented positive outcomes within inclusive public education experiences that will be explored later in this book.

QUESTIONS FOR REFLECTION

- Are any of the statistics in this chapter surprising?
- What is a reasonable number of students with learning disabilities in a classroom that will maintain a balance and reflect general society?
- What is the balance in each classroom in my school?
- Which are the most common disabilities in my school? How do I know this OR how can I find out if I don't know?
- How well equipped are the teachers in my school to teach the disabilities of our students?

CHAPTER 3:
ASSESSING THE SITUATION

Whatever you have learned or received
or heard from me, or seen in me—put it into practice.
And the God of peace will be with you.

PHILIPPIANS 4:9

Assessing the Situation

The following assessments are meant to help school leadership determine where to begin the process of building capacity among staff and building a program for exceptional learners. If decisions are to be made based on this information, it will be important for teachers and staff to feel comfortable being honest. Creating an opportunity as early on in the process as possible to gather information will likely provide the most accurate results.

Invite all teaching faculty, aides, and staff members to participate in the surveys so you can get a read on the entire pool of school employees. Staff will be called on in different ways than teachers, but their knowledge and dispositions especially will be critical to the success of students with special needs and their parents. School restrooms may need to be modified by janitorial or facilities staff to accommodate wheelchairs, communications and marketing directors will need to consider person-first language and the use of diverse photography to represent the school community online and in print materials. A health aide or nurse may need to provide medications or other treatments to students who have disabilities, receptionists and front office personnel may greet students and families upon arrival at school, and school counselors or guidance counselors are working to develop the academic pathways that students will follow. Each must demonstrate the appropriate knowledge, skills, and dispositions to help all students. Having the involvement of all staff unites the community.

Suggestions for Assessment Distribution

At the beginning of the school year, perhaps your first training or schoolwide faculty meeting, consider distributing these self-assessments of the knowledge, skills and dispositions of your faculty and staff anonymously. The self-assessment of knowledge considers what each person knows about disabilities such as dyslexia, ADHD, speech and language impairments, etc. Perhaps he or she knows a child with autism and has a frame of reference but does not yet know how this disability can impact a child's learning in the classroom. The self-assessment of skills considers the teaching skills necessary to educate different learners and create a learning space that is sensitive to all ability levels. Dispositions are assessed based upon the tenets of Catholic social teaching. Teachers will identify their personal beliefs aligned with Catholic social teaching that are inherent within our faith and mission of Catholic education.

This is your baseline, the knowledge, skills, and dispositions that your faculty and staff possess at the onset of the school year. Allow time between the baseline survey and a follow up before asking people to commit to their answers by identifying themselves. Your whole-faculty baseline must be an accurate and true reflection of the culture, climate, and community. Following the assessment tables are scenarios that may be helpful to determine a course of action.

TABLE 3

SELF-ASSESSMENT OF KNOWLEDGE

	Not Yet	Getting Started	On the way	Refining
I feel confident addressing the traits of the diagnosis of autism has on a student's ability to learn.				
I feel confident addressing the traits of the diagnosis of dyslexia has on a student's ability to learn.				
I feel confident addressing the traits of the diagnosis of ADHD has on a student's ability to learn.				
I feel confident addressing the traits of the diagnosis of executive function disorder has on a student's ability to learn.				
I feel confident addressing the traits of the diagnosis of orthopedic impairment has on a student's ability to learn.				
I feel confident addressing the traits of the diagnosis of intellectual disability has on a student's ability to learn.				
I feel confident addressing the traits of the diagnosis of dyscalculia has on a student's ability to learn.				
I feel confident addressing the traits of the diagnosis of speech and language impairment has on a student's ability to learn.				

TABLE 3.1

SELF-ASSESSMENT OF SKILLS

	Not Yet	Getting Started	On the way	Refining
I apply evidence-based strategies to teach students who learn differently due to a disability.				
I develop accommodations and modifications to my teaching, assignments, and assessments to lessen the impact of a disability in my classroom.				
I am comfortable using several methods of assessment to assess learning, including but not limited to: online modalities, oral presentations, videos, group projects, and interviews.				
I focus on the essential learning targets of a given assignment, task, assessment, or project to assess understanding of critical concepts.				
I apply principles of Universal Design for Learning consistently to increase access to curriculum for all learners.				
My classroom is a welcome environment where tolerance, understanding, and respect is demonstrated by all students.				
I know how to create a safe environment for asking questions, seeking out additional assistance, and using accommodations.				
I implement a positive behavior system in my classroom.				
I address the learning differences inherent in the classroom, supporting the students who struggle as well as those who need accelerated curriculum.				

TABLE 3.2

SELF-ASSESSMENT OF DISPOSITIONS

	Not Yet	Getting Started	On the way	Refining
I am committed to providing all students the opportunity for a Catholic education.				
I believe that every person is precious, that people are more important than things, and that the measure of every institution is whether it threatens or enhances the life and dignity of the human person.				
I believe people have a right and a duty to participate in society, seeking together the common good and well-being of all, especially the poor and vulnerable.				
I believe we are one human family whatever our national, racial, ethnic, economic, and ideological differences. We are our brothers and sisters keepers, wherever they may be.				
I believe we are called to protect people and the planet, living our faith in relationship with all of God's creation.				
I believe in my responsibility to others, to our families, and to the larger society.				
I believe all persons share in and contribute to the common good.				

Course of Action

While we wish there were an algorithm to predict the exactly correct way to respond to the results obtained, the following scenarios may provide some structure for your next steps. Consider your data once the self-assessments have been completed. Using the self-assessment for knowledge, skills, and dispositions, you can tally responses for each prompt to learn where your faculty and staff have strengths and areas to focus on. No two schools are the same, so no canned response will solve all of the issues leaders face in the early stages of this process. Keep the data so that you can compare as your program grows year to year.

Here are some scenarios to guide your thinking:

TABLE 3.3

If the data indicates:	K=Knowledge; S=Skills; D=Dispositions Consider these activities:
Not Yet Knowledge Not Yet Skills Not Yet Dispositions	**K:** Begin conversations with your staff about disability awareness. Share information from websites such as the National Center for Learning Disabilities, Autism Speaks, the American Speech, Language, Hearing Association and others where facts, resources, and information can be found. **S:** Develop a Professional Learning Community (PLC) focused on building the skills of your educators in the areas of data collection and analysis, differentiated instruction, Universal Design for Learning, and building positive behavioral supports throughout campus. Reach out to your community and larger diocese for professional development opportunities, guest speakers, and mentor teachers. **D:** Read your school mission and vision statements; Do they include the mission of the Church to educate all of God's children? If not, build consensus among your faculty and staff to add inclusive language to your mission and vision. Review Catholic social teaching and *Ensuring a Place at the Table*
Refining Knowledge Refining Skills Not Yet Dispositions	**K and S:** Continue to address knowledge and skills across school wide professional development programs. Ensure that these efforts are not dependent upon an individual, but rather the community. **D:** Go back to the mission- establish the **WHY** Incorporate Catholic social teaching into trainings, conversations, and rationales Use language that refers to the dignity of all persons Review Church documents, like the *Pastoral Statement of the Catholic Bishops on Persons with Disabilities* (1978) or the 2017 white paper release by NCEA, *One Spirit, One Church*

Getting Started with Knowledge Not Yet for Skills On the Way for Dispositions	**K:** Address the professional development program for the school year and beyond Consider National Catholic Educational Association (NCEA), Mustard Seed, Foundation for Inclusive Religious Education (FIRE) conference, regional conferences focused on inclusive practices, and local state department of education trainings. Encourage teachers to take classes to learn about specific topics, such as autism, dyslexia, ADHD, or anxiety disorders. **S:** Use Title funds to bring in a coach to work with teachers in their classrooms to refine skills for teaching a diversified group of learners. Hire a special educator Explore a co-teaching model with special education teachers and general classroom teachers **D:** You already have the **WHY** agreed upon, continue to share this message.
Not Yet/ Getting Started with Knowledge Refining Skills Getting Started with Dispositions	**K:** Teacher mentoring program - you have great teachers! Let them partner with colleagues! Teach them how what they do works for exceptional learners. Training for disability awareness. Start with the teachers who have specific students in their classrooms, move to school-wide initiative **S:** Implement a process for teachers to share their skills with new teachers, specialty area teachers, and staff as needed. Consider the skills that can continue to grow and be supported. **D:** Continue to build dispositions, the **WHY** is part of every program on campus. Conversations about inclusion are specific and have the intention to build upon the momentum established.

On the Way for Knowledge Getting Started with Skills Refining for Dispositions	**K:** Build upon the strengths of faculty knowledge, share this during training and group learning opportunities. **S:** Address differentiated instruction and Universal Design for Learning (UDL) specifically for exceptional learners through professional development Begin a teacher mentoring program, pair experienced teachers with novices to support exceptional learners Integrate skills needed to accommodate and modify lessons to teacher observations and evaluations Address behavioral supports as a campus-wide initiative if not already in place **D:** Reinforce the Catholic disposition of the school in all classrooms and activities
On the Way for Knowledge On the Way for Skills On the Way for Dispositions	**KSD:** You have a solid foundation across your faculty and staff. Dig deeper into the data! Consider patterns in the responses: What knowledge is missing (autism, orthopedic impairment, etc.)? What skills need refining? What principles of Catholic social justice need some refining? Focus your professional development calendar on the specific areas for refining and embed skills such as differentiation and UDL across all training areas Implement mentoring where needed Create a Community of Practice or PLC to support inclusive practices across campus programs Implement marketing strategies to increase your population of exceptional learners Align activities to administrative and diocesan efforts to become more inclusive Consider partnering with a school to support their inclusive efforts – teaching others often leads to more learning!

QUESTIONS FOR REFLECTION

- What stands out among the responses from the self-assessments?
- Considering the ratings on the "Knowledge" assessment, what trainings will be necessary?
- Considering the ratings on the "Skills" assessment, what trainings will be necessary?
- Considering the ratings on the "Dispositions" assessment, what trainings will be necessary?
- Are resources readily available for these trainings?
- Do you feel you need to collect more data before moving forward?

Chapter 4:
Blueprint for Building:
A Program Framework

*That same day Jesus went out of the house and sat beside the sea.
And great crowds gathered about him, so that he got into a boat
and sat down. And the whole crowd stood on the beach. And he
told them many things in parables, saying: "A sower went out to
sow. And as he sowed, some seeds fell along the path, and the birds
came and devoured them. Other seeds fell on rocky ground, where
they did not have much soil, and immediately they sprang up,
since they had no depth of soil ...*

Matthew 13:1-5

Where to Begin...

Once the need for a program is established among the community, the question becomes—
How do we do it? Once people commit, they will want to know where to start. Planners
among the group will want to know the timeline, the goals, and the expectations of leadership. It's a lot to think about! Just remember, rocky ground is an excellent starting point for
bearing the most glorious fruit! Every aspect of a plan does not have to be in place before
you begin. In fact, the early stages of program establishment will be about building capacity
—and will likely be a little messy.

While this framework provides some long-range projections of what a program can
eventually become, it is important to take adequate time with each aspect and stage. The
time frame for moving from the preparation stage to reaching Level 1 and passing on to
Level 2 is not important. Different communities will take more time than others for very
different reasons. Being thorough and deliberate with each aspect at the outset will bear
fruit in the long run. Program development is a journey, most definitely not a race.

Level Descriptions

Level 1 Schools are in the early stages of program development. Everything feels exploratory and experimental as trial and error may be the norm for establishing procedures and protocols. Data does not drive instruction, and accommodations and modifications are not widely used or well understood. The graphics and tables below will provide more specifics.

Level 2 Schools have established programs, program directors, staff fully on board, and several effective practices in place as well as communities that are open to inclusive practices. Teachers receive training and are provided resources to meet a variety of student learning needs. More specifics are provided later in this chapter.

Level 3 Schools have strong, well established programs that support a variety of learning challenges, embedded teacher training and support in place, and communities that understand that including diversified learners is good for the whole community as well as a significant part of living our Catholic mission in education. These schools have partnerships with their local public schools and other community organizations to support the needs of their students. A continuous improvement cycle exists to maintain an excellent program. Keep reading for more details on Level 3 schools!

A Framework for Level 1, 2, and 3 Schools

The following breakdowns of Level 1, 2, and 3 School programs are more clearly established in the tables found later in this chapter. However, these graphics provide a snapshot of aspects found at basic, intermediate, and advanced stages of program establishment.

TABLE 4

Little knowledge of specific, common learning disabilities or diagnoses that affect student learning	No designated staff for students with disabilities (resource teacher, reading interventionist, or special education teacher) to handle caseload of students who need accommodations, student support plans, or modifications	Minimal if any professional development for teaching students with disabilities has occurred

LEVEL 1 SCHOOLS

Uncertainty with how to develop student support plans from an MET or IEP or as need is indicated	In the first few years of program development Minimal or basic student achievement data	Support students with diagnoses or disabilities on a case by case basis because little or no clear parameters for admissions

**Most schools can move on to Level 2 once they establish some intentional systems and hire a person to lead the program. Moving to Level 2 means community outreach has occurred, and parents are working with parish and school leadership toward productive program development.

TABLE 4.1

Established systems are in place for students with special needs, and all school personnel are aware School culture has made progress in welcoming and belonging for all people.	Leadership team has a firm understanding of the school's capabilities and limitations for educating students with learning challenges, physical disabilities, or health impairments or other diagnoses that affect learning (usually because of previous experiences).	Dedicated physical space for the Program Coordinator to work in Excellent data is used to understand student learning growth or skill gaps, and progress is monitored for all students.

LEVEL 2 SCHOOLS

Financial resources exist for teachers to receive training or coaching for teaching students with disabilities or other diagnoses.	Teachers use a Care Team or other teacher assistance team regularly to help one another work through student issues. The school community is supportive and understanding of students who have more moderate to severe disabilities.	A dedicated staff person handles all student support plans and assists teachers with accommodations and interventions in the classroom.

**Most schools remain in Level 2 until a solid program is established, professional development is ongoing and embedded, and school/community culture is welcoming and inclusive. Complacency can lead to backslide if the program is not maintained. A plan for program maintenance should be part of schools' continuous improvement cycles so that it remains a priority. A school is ready for Level 3 when the program is an embedded part of school culture.

TABLE 4.2

Teachers are well supported and continuously trained or coached to work with the students in their classrooms.

Solid relationships exist with community resources to support the school for success with a diverse variety of learners.

The program director or coordinator works in tandem with the principal but takes the lead on all special education issues.

LEVEL 3 SCHOOLS

These schools become an exemplary model of inclusive efforts, may take on the role of mentors and/or trainers to lower level schools, and may be active in professional development workshops.

Established admissions process is in place to admit students with high incidence and low incidence disabilities based on clear parameters and partnerships with families.

**Schools in Level 3 show their Catholic Identity through exemplifying a true call to Catholic mission.

A Note on Fluctuation Between Levels

We can always hope that once a program is established, it will remain and only get stronger. However, schools depend on people to function. As people change, so might any established programs. With a change of leadership or faculty turnover, a school can revert from Level 2 to Level 1 or Level 3 to Level 2 at any given time. Re-establish the parameters of the program or the culture through training, setting clear expectations, or providing general professional development.

The Framework

TABLE 4.3

	Level 1	Level 2	Level 3
Determine Disposition (leadership, faculty, staff, community)	Assess attitudes toward inclusive education practices. (Options for assessment are provided.)	School personnel understand the connection between Catholic social teaching and the provision of services to students with disabilities.	Strong involvement of shareholders exemplifies Catholic social teaching in action through services to students with disabilities; all members of the community are personally committed to success for all students.
Identification (of students and learning needs)	Universal screener in place; data on all students' academic achievement is accessible.	Universal screener is used by teachers to group students for differentiated instruction and assessment.	Universal screener is used by all teachers to group students for differentiated instruction and assessment.
Procedures and Responsibilities (of faculty) — Accommodations	Teachers learn and employ basic accommodations according to the student support plan in place.	Teachers try various interventions and employ accommodations as needed based on progress monitoring data.	Teachers demonstrate a clear understanding of interventions, accommodations, and modifications and are comfortable implementing each.
Procedures and Responsibilities (of faculty) — Focused, Appropriate Instruction	Teachers utilize differentiated instruction to meet the needs of various types of learners.	Teachers naturally utilize differentiated instruction and assessment to reach students and determine whether/how well they have learned skills and concepts.	All teachers have a firm understanding of multiple intelligences, know the types of learning styles of their students, and teach and assess using multiple modalities.
Procedures and Responsibilities (of faculty)— Data Analyses	Teachers communicate with each other to analyze student data and share teaching strategies.	Grade level and/or grade band teams meet regularly to formally discuss student growth data, including identification of skill and knowledge gaps and teaching strategies; teams discuss differentiated assessments and assessment strategies.	Teacher teams are part of the professional culture of the school. Teachers are comfortable analyzing, sharing, and problem-solving through student data. Team time is maximized, formalized, and protected.

Admissions Process	Process in place to collect information from parents and other schools, if appropriate, for students with already identified needs. School makes determinations on what resources are needed to educate the student.	Student Support Personnel participate in admissions interviews to gather specific information on the resources and accommodations necessary to educate the student.	Student Support Personnel participate in admissions interviews to understand learning needs and make determinations on how to educate the student AND whether/which outside agencies can be partners in supporting the student through additional services (in partnership with the LEA and/or family).
Functional Operation (for continuous progress)	Students with high incidence disabilities are identified and assisted in the classroom. A student support plan is developed and shared with teachers.	Students needing extra support meet with the student support teacher/ resource teacher as needed. Community exhibits openness to students with lower incidence disabilities. Student support plan is developed by teachers and parents and implemented.	Students with high incidence disabilities are identified and assisted quickly by classroom teachers; school has shown success with students with lower incidence disabilities. Team-developed student support plans are implemented and monitored by the resource teacher or program director.
Functional Operation (for continuous progress)	Develop communication standards for administration, teachers, and parents to establish partnership around a student's educational needs.	Foster communication among student support teacher, classroom teacher, administration, and parents to remain proactive regarding student needs. Communication with community and diocesan contacts are utilized.	Foster communication among student support teacher, classroom teacher, administration, and parents to remain proactive regarding student needs. Progress is clearly measured and communicated. Communication with community and diocesan contacts are utilized as needed.

General Program Components	Teachers demonstrate good teaching strategies and learn about interventions, accommodations, and modifications.	Dedicated resource teacher supervises Program for Diversified Learners and acts as the primary contact for LEA, classroom teachers, Care Team, and parents of students with support plans; teacher has working knowledge of special education law and how it relates to Catholic schools.	There is a Program Director for the Diversified Learner Program that is regarded and involved as an administrator. This person provides coaching, training, resources,and helps teacher teams monitor student progress. The Program Director is well connected with other Support Personnel in the diocese and with community members.
Professional Development	Time and resources are dedicated to PD in the areas of differentiated instruction and teaching strategies for students with high incidence disabilities.	Principal and resource teacher determine clear areas of need (skills and knowledge) and find appropriate, directed professional development.	School, principal, and teachers become mentors/trainers; possibly even become PD speakers and help provide trainings to others. They seek out professional development opportunities and model best practices.
Community Partnerships	Relationships begin to develop between school and local organizations to assist with student support and teacher professional development. The school may need to make intentional outreach efforts to connect with local agencies.	Relationships with local partners are established. School helps parents connect with local professionals that can provide services not available at school. Appropriate measures are taken to incorporate therapies or tutoring into the schedule as needed for some students.	Many community/local partnerships exist to help families outside of school, provide services during or after school hours, and to provide consultation and professional assistance to teachers as needed.

Schools:
- should be flexible. If a student is admitted, the school should fulfill the appropriate accommodations or modifications for that student. A one-size-fits-all approach to accommodations is not appropriate.
- should not admit a student without meeting the parents and the student first. Making a sound decision includes seeing all testing documents and previous accommodation documents (IEPs, ISPs, SSPs, etc.) and interacting with all members of the

family to inform the decision. Speaking with a child's previous school can give you an idea of how the child will function best in your school as well as the strengths of the family in terms of collaboration, support, and communication.

- should not place a student in the back of the room with his or her aide to do independent teaching for the majority of the day and call it inclusion. If a student is accepted into a school, his/her academic, social, spiritual, and emotional health and growth must all be addressed and efforts must be made to mainstream when possible. Co-teaching is an option in these situations.

SPOTLIGHT ON ST. ANN SCHOOL

A wonderful, well-loved principal retired after more than 26 years on the job, leaving his Catholic school in the hands of two brand new administrators. The new principal and assistant principal quickly realized a few things about their faculty. There had been very little turnover throughout the years, so the teachers were firmly rooted in their community but also in their roles, structures, habits—and silos!

A new initiative was put in place. The assistant principal was asked by the principal to gather data on students with learning disabilities and any who might be falling through the cracks. For years, the faculty dealt with each student's challenges individually. In the culture of this faculty, handling your own student issues was a show of strength. As such, there were few reports to administration about challenges in the classroom, few referrals for testing, no formal documentation, and no opportunity for vertical communication between teachers, as students moved from one grade level to the next, to share ideas on how to best reach those students who had learning difficulties.

On the faculty, there was no reading specialist or interventionist of any kind, there had been no professional development on teaching students with disabilities, and no formal process in place for addressing common learning challenges with effective interventions or accommodations. The assistant principal attended a diocesan training on forming Teacher Assistance Teams within a school to create a culture of support around both teachers and students and saw her opportunity to try this approach at St. Ann's. She read the book *The Care Team Approach* and began the implementation process at her first opportunity. She gave teachers permission to open up about challenges with students in their classrooms by coming to a structured Care Team meeting and presenting their situations to one another. Together, the teachers solved problems, shared ideas, and supported students and peers alike. Teachers were validated and empowered, often surprising themselves with their expertise on how to work with students with learning and behavioral challenges.

A process was put in place for teachers to petition to bring a case to the Care Team, documentation processes were established, and the assistant principal took on the role of coordinating Student Support Plan meetings between teachers and parents of students who had learning disabilities, health issues that affected learning, and those struggling enough to need accommodations and explore formal testing.

It took one year to get these structures in place at St. Ann's. Four years later, there is a reading specialist, a math interventionist, and a speech therapist on staff. St. Ann's is a Level 1 school moving closer to Level 2.

QUESTIONS FOR REFLECTION

- How will I know my school community is ready for the Program Development phase?
- What would my school community's year one plan and goals be?
- Which areas of the Framework will my community have the most success achieving or developing?
- Which areas will give us the most challenge?
- What resources will my community need most immediately to help us get started?

CHAPTER 5:
THE ROLE OF LEADERSHIP

And let us not grow weary of doing good,
for in due season we will reap, if we do not give up.
GALATIANS 6:9

"As the Leader Goes, So Goes the People"

The importance of a school's leadership cannot be overstated when it comes to setting the stage for exceptional learner programs. Many schools have leadership teams that include pastors, assistant principals, teacher leaders, or directors. For the sake of understanding this chapter, the leader is the principal of the school.

Development of an exceptional learner program takes dedication and passion, and the leader may need to climb a mountain if the situation calls for it. The challenges that come with this project are unique. The hearts and minds of people you thought you knew well may be revealed in unexpected ways. As the leader, approach any change by first understanding the hurdles your faculty, staff, and general community will undergo through the process. Some of those hurdles will be learning challenges while others may be emotional hurdles.

Holding people to the expectation to walk the talk of one's stated beliefs can create a shift in the balance. Some teachers will joyfully respond with, "It's about time!" Others will be cautious but open, while some may react with outright opposition. Leaders should be prepared for every emotion to be revealed and ready to allow people to process information openly. Just do not allow emotion to derail the process. Fear is often at the heart of oppositional responses, and fear can be overcome. Logically, philosophically, and theologically speaking, Catholic schools should never have excluded exceptional learners. By our mission, it is a very basic expectation. Creating communities of belonging for exceptional learners in a Catholic school community that has previously not had a program in place should be welcomed. Our belief as Catholics is, of course, that every person is a child of God, created in His image. Cling to the virtues of faith, hope, charity, justice, and fortitude to keep people focused. We cannot teach these virtues yet not practice them, after all.

It is human nature to revert to personal experiences, biases, and judgements when facing a change; and change does not always bring out the best in us--at first. Often a first response to any suggested change to the norm is, "This won't work." Or, "We already tried this."

By their nature, good leaders are able to see past immediate obstacles and keep an eye on the ultimate goal. When the goal is truly fulfilling Catholic mission in education, we cannot afford to succumb to resistance.

ADMINISTRATOR RESPONSIBILITIES

In the beginning, developing a program for exceptional learners lies on the shoulders of the principal. Leadership is paramount to the successful process of transforming the minds and hearts of teachers as well as preparing them with skills and knowledge. Preparing a community for the success of any new program also takes intentionality and care.

The principal:

- must evaluate the pulse of the community and respond to dispositions appropriately by forming other administrators, teachers, staff, students, and families to be open and welcoming.
- must be the program's cheerleader and agent by leading in word and action.
- must be able to defend the Catholic church's mission and the role of education in it.
- must be willing to take risks.
- must hire people who believe in the mission of Catholic education.
- must understand the basics of IDEA, as it applies to private schools.
- MUST inherently believe that all children can learn and that, through strong family partnerships, almost any student can receive a Catholic education.

TABLE 5

# The Principal

The program's cheerleader and agent who leads in word and action.	Hires people who believe in the mission of Catholic education.	Defends the Catholic church's mission and the role of education in it.
Evaluate the pulse of the community and respond to dispositions appropriately by forming other administrators, teachers, staff, students, and families to be open and welcoming.	MUST inherently believe that all children can learn and that, through strong family partnership, almost any student can receive a Catholic education.	

TABLE 5.1

	Level 1	Level 2	Level 3
Administrator Responsibilities: **Catholic Mission**	Educate faculty on school mission, Catholic mission, and set clear expectations. Use church documents to help build the foundation of understanding the purpose of Catholic schools.	Administration leads education of school community on Catholic mission and how it applies to welcoming and educating all families who seek a Catholic education.	Catholic mission in education is understood by school and parish families because the administrator sets the example and expectations. A sense of belonging exists for all families, and trusted partnerships exist between families and school administration.
Policy Guidance	Familiarize all faculty members with diocesan guidance (Guidebook, Handbook or policies) regarding diversified learners. (If there is no guidebook from the diocese, begin the conversation to develop one.)	Faithfully use policies, procedures, documents, and available diocesan guidance to create clear, consistent program processes documentation.	Monitor comfortability and use of appropriate policies, procedures and documentation to ensure consistency and comfortability by all faculty and staff.
Programming	Make a plan to develop a program for diversified learners that is overseen by designated personnel. The principal may have to drive the process early on, but delegating will become necessary fairly quickly.	Administrative duties for the oversight of the planned exceptional learner program are entrusted to designated, qualified personnel.	Student support personnel act as school administration, overseeing the exceptional learner program. Principal is kept informed on any significant issues regarding exceptional learners.
Inventory	Analyze faculty inventory results to understand knowledge, skills, and dispositions. Make a plan to address needs and utilize strengths.	Give yearly inventory of knowledge skills and dispositions so that response (in the form of communications, trainings, etc.) is always relevant.	Administration ensures that teachers have easy access to resources that will help them meet the needs of their students in terms of trainings, equipment, consultants, therapists, etc.

Relationship with Local Education Agency (LEA)	Develop a relationship with special education liaison in your LEA .	Relationship with LEA is strong between administration/ student support personnel. IDEA and legal rights for students with disabilities are understood by administration/student support person and employed appropriately for qualified students.	Relationship with LEA is strong between administration / student support personnel. IDEA and legal rights for students with disabilities are understood and well- articulated by administration /student support person and employed appropriately for qualified students.
Professional Development	Dedicate time and resources to PD of teachers and aides.	Ensure PD for teachers is current and addresses the needs of the students they teach. Be sure to address gaps in knowledge and skills according to inventory data.	Time, budget, and relevant PD is sacred and protected.
Student Support Team (SST) also called Care Teams	Learn about Care Teams/ Teacher Assistance teams. Make a Care Team part of your program plan.	Develop a student support team (Care Team, etc.) and a clear process for referral. Be part of the Care Team until you are satisfied with its functionality.	Student support team is part of school culture and is facilitated by the student support coordinator.

A Note on Admissions and Relationships

Sometimes, because parents of children with disabilities feel stigmatized by schools that have an admissions process, openness about having an IEP or a specific diagnosis is held back. If we want parents to be open about their children's needs, their first contact with the school and most definitely their conversation with the admissions coordinator must be a positive experience. Unfortunately, most Catholic schools have a stigma of being private and exclusive so parents are not always forthcoming with a diagnosis or an IEP. There are legitimate reasons for this. A negative perception has been created by Catholic schools that have operated as private and exclusive and have, perhaps, told families that children with disabilities would be better served in public school. Yes, it's true… we did this to ourselves. How do we mitigate the damage?

Schools have amazed themselves with success stories of educating students with moderate to severe disabilities. In our experience, we have witnessed that it is rarely the mildness or the severity of the disability that impacts a school's ability to educate a child. The one factor that consistently seems to make or break a student's success is the relationship between the family and the school. Trust must exist for the child to succeed at school. The family must trust that the school loves and supports its students and that school personnel will do everything in their power to help the student achieve his/her goals, whether social, emotional, academic, or spiritual. A school must be able to trust that the family is following through with agreed upon structures at home and that the student is receiving any necessary outside therapies, tutoring, or counseling that is not provided by the school.

High school principals and admissions directors must be on the same page when it comes to being open to admitting students with special needs. Many families have experienced a number of successful years at a Catholic elementary school for their special needs child only to be told that the local Catholic high school is "only college prep," or "there is a school down the street with an appropriate program for you," or "we only make one kind of accommodation, so you'll have to work around us if you want to come here," or "we've had experiences with other kids with special needs that just didn't work out and we don't want that to happen again." These are statements made by schools that take an ad hoc approach to serving students with disabilities. There are simply too many success stories of exceptional learners in Catholic high schools to say that students with special needs just don't belong or cannot succeed there. Universities and colleges across the country have supports put in place built around assistive technology, UDL, and training for professors who have been taught and held accountable to making accommodations for students. As college prep schools, Catholic high schools can look to higher education to learn how to teach college-bound students with special needs.

On another note, for students with more severe disabilities who may not be able to complete, for example, the math track in a college prep school or may be unable to read at the high school level, developing individualized programs and creating a four-year plan with specific goals in order to earn a state diploma or a certificate of completion from a Catholic high school is a viable alternative. It takes willingness and creativity, a good working relationship with the parents, and a plan.

Hiring for Mission

When the opportunity arises to hire new teachers, intentionality in measuring each candidate's knowledge, skills, and dispositions with regard to exceptional learners must be part of the process. Hiring is a learned skill in and of itself, and every hire is an unknown entity. However, making decisions based on clear organizational goals and objectives, needs and philosophies, and core Catholic values will help the best candidates for a school rise to the surface.

Strategic interview questions can help leaders meet their personnel needs. These are a few examples to demonstrate the differences between questions to help determine Knowledge, Skills, and Disposition. Being intentional about identifying where people fall on the spectrum of these areas will likely help determine whether a candidate will be a good fit for your community.

Experienced leaders or those who have participated on hiring committees may recognize some of these questions as common questions to use when screening candidates. As a leader's or hiring committee's focus shifts to hiring candidates with the appropriate Knowledge, Skills, and Dispositions to meet the needs of the school community, the answers take a different shape and bring a new meaning and purpose to the interview process.

TABLE 5.2

CATEGORY	QUESTION	INTERPRETATION
KNOWLEDGE	What are some data points you use to help plan your lessons?	Asking this question will let you know whether the person uses data to guide instruction and monitor student performance. He or she should be able to articulate their understanding of students' reading abilities, for example, based on a variety of data points.
KNOWLEDGE	What professional development have you received in the area of teaching students with disabilities?	This will give information on a couple of points. First, it tells whether and how much professional development has occurred on special education topics for this candidate. You will also be able to learn whether the candidate knows the difference between learning disabilities and other diagnoses, such autism, ADHD, or other health issues that might require a student support plan. How well he or she articulates background knowledge specifically on learning disabilities will help interviewers gauge Knowledge. Pay attention to HOW the candidate speaks about his or her training on learning disabilities, too. You would need to consider the fit of a candidate that may be dismissive of the need for knowledge of learning disabilities.
SKILLS	When your first attempt at teaching a concept doesn't work for the majority of the class, what do you do next? What if it still isn't sticking for a few students? What do you do for them?	A candidate with the skills to teach a diverse community of learners will have a deep toolbox of teaching techniques. This question will allow a candidate to draw on his or her experience or training to reason through the process. In the case of a new teacher with limited classroom experience, even a theoretical answer will show whether he or she would know how to handle such a scenario. Listen for answers that include use of interventions, varied assessments, approaches to reaching visual, auditory, or other types of learners. Strong skills include an understanding of differentiated instruction, re-teaching through chunking material, and ability to adjust the content and delivery of a lesson, how a student demonstrates learning, and the creation of an environment that is flexible and safe for a variety of learners.

SKILLS	How do you know all of your students are learning? What do you do for those who are moving quickly through material? Moving slowly through material?	Answers to this question can come in many forms, from, "I just know," to "I use daily assessments to measure growth." In a highly diversified community of learners, the skill to be able to assess students' progress through a specific measurement mechanism is going to be important. A candidate's experience in the classroom will come through in this answer, as he or she will have the opportunity to recall how and when they actually provided intervention in both scenarios. The candidate's openness to students on both ends of the learning spectrum will also likely come through. It is hard to hide the genuine joy of breaking through a student's barrier to learning or the excitement of helping a student soar ahead in the same way it is hard to disguise frustration for students who cannot keep up or want to race ahead of the planned lessons. This answer straddles both Skills and Dispositions.
DISPOSITION	As part of the admissions committee at this school, what factors would be important to you for families/students seeking admittance?	Catholic schools are sometimes misperceived as exclusive, PRIVATE schools. Because we are Catholic first, understanding our mission of evangelization is key to being open to partnering with families to prepare their children–even if those children have learning challenges or physical disabilities. A candidate's response to this question will reveal his or her belief in inclusive practices, how they value diversity, and whether they believe there are students who should not be admitted.
DISPOSITION	If I were to tell you the class you're being hired for has at least 10 students with learning challenges, what questions or concerns would you have?	This question will open the door to a potentially great conversation. The candidate's first response, of course, will tell so much. A smile? A drop of the jaw? A widening of the eyes and a "Whew!" What follows the initial response can show depth of understanding if he or she asks questions, for example, about the types of learning challenges, resources available, and how the previous year's teacher succeeded with the students. Other questions might focus on who pulls the students out of class for intervention or whether there is a person on staff that helps with students with special needs. Regardless of whether the response is a list of questions, concerns, or examples of how the person would get to know each student and meet their needs, this question will likely reveal where the person lands on the disposition spectrum.

These are examples of questions to use for strategic interviewing. No matter the questions used to screen candidates, consider what types of answers you would like to hear from potential employees before the interview begins. There is a science to hiring. The more structured the process and the more objective the leader or committee making the decisions, the more likely you will find the right candidate. The right teachers make all the difference, as research has proven time and again that the teacher makes the greatest impact in a child's learning.

As your school moves beyond Level 1 status, you may become sensitive to person first language when interviewing candidates. Candidates who refer to individuals by their disability are not using person-first language, they are labeling a student based upon a characteristic. An example of person-first language would be "a student with dyslexia" or "a student with a vision impairment" rather than a dyslexic or blind student. Just as we would not label students based upon cultural, ethnic, or physical traits, we would not label them by disability.

Finally, place high importance on checking references. Wanting to believe all that your top candidates say in the interview can impede diligent follow up. (Been there, made that mistake!) Because teachers have the greatest impact on students, cutting corners in the hiring process can cause leaders to kick themselves partway through the year. Following a clear, objective, and consistent process for each and every candidate, whether it is someone known to the community or not, is equally important. Hire with confidence.

This chapter places a great deal of weight on the school leader. Stay the course and be strengthened by your purpose to do God's work. As you hire staff specifically for developing and leading this work, do not be tempted to leave it in the care of another without accountability. Your commitment to serving all students supports all members of your faculty and staff to stay the course. Leading with the intention to do what is best for the students God has placed in your care will be your greatest challenge and greatest reward.

The first section of this chapter paves the road for leadership components of program development and is followed by suggestions for choosing collaborators and teammates. The next chapter will explore program implementation. Once a leader has committed, created a vision, and chosen a team, the program can move forward.

QUESTIONS FOR REFLECTION

- What are the strengths of my school's principal that will bolster support for a program for exceptional learners at my school?
- What are my principal's limitations? Who on staff has the skills to fill those gaps?
- For a parent of a child with exceptional learning needs, is the first conversation with school personnel about their child positive and welcoming?
- If my school's principal takes on all of the responsibilities in the Level I chart of Administrator Responsibilities, what tasks can other school staff take on to create some balance of duties?

Chapter 6:
Implementation

Don't you be afraid, for I am with you. Don't be dismayed,
for I am your God. I will strengthen you. Yes, I will help you.
Yes, I will uphold you with the right hand of my righteousness.
Isaiah 41:10

The Nike Corporation is known for the trademark phrase "Just Do It." This essentially means that you should not let challenges, barriers, or excuses prevent greatness. Whether training to run a marathon or preparing to change the schoolwide culture to become more inclusive, the education leader ultimately must decide to "Just Do It." The Why do it is what you have already established individually or as a school and makes pieces fall into place once you establish the importance of an inclusive Catholic environment. The How cripples our good intentions. Change is hard, however we have science that is research based and process oriented to support our efforts. This does not mean that it will be easy, happen quickly, or be perfectly designed without error; rather it provides a blueprint for success that we can adapt for the unique demographics on a given campus.

> *"Behavior precedes belief - that is, most people must engage in a behavior before they accept that it is beneficial; then they see the results, and then they believe that it is the right thing to do....implementation precedes buy-in; it does not follow it."*
> —Douglas B. Reeves

The process by which change occurs must be purposeful and the educational leaders resolute in efforts to work through the adaptive and technical challenges that will arise. The challenges that will be encountered are considered adaptive and technical. Adaptive challenges defined by Blase, Fixsen, Sims, and Ward (2015) are those which cause the leaders and educators to revise and rethink core values, beliefs, and the "way we have always done it." Challenges that are technical in nature are not easier to overcome, however they may be addressed through policy set forth by leadership (Blase, et al., 2015). Schedule, class size, room allocation, staffing, etc. are intimidating challenges, however the solutions come about through typical school process. Adaptive challenges often result in feelings of fear, incompetence, or grief for the comfortable past (Blase, et al., 2015). These challenges are normal and to be expected; they will not prevent the "Just Do It" attitude or realization that the outcomes are worthy of the fears, stress, and hard work.

Implementation is a Science

Implementation is defined in this context by Fixsen, (2005, p.5) as "a specified set of activities designed to put into practice an activity or program of known dimensions." The educational leaders' plan is comprised of activities or tasks that will be put into practice to bring about an inclusive school environment for exceptional learners. Our intent is not to make you an expert in implementation science, rather to share the basic structure so that you can see the path forward and know your desired outcome is possible. This is not light work, and it requires a willingness to make mistakes. For more detailed information, the National Implementation Research Network (NIRN) is a wonderful resource to explore.

Program Development and Implementation Process

Good intentions are not enough to affect change in a school. You could likely recall several programs and initiatives that were tried for a period of time and then discontinued for one reason or another. When you consider the time, resources, and funds used and perhaps ultimately wasted, an implementation plan should seem quite appealing. Your implementation plan will depend upon the program and level you identify with in the Program Framework and rubric.

Implementation can be thought of as a process of continuous improvement. You will repeat stages and stay in one stage for a long period of time. The stages guide the establishment of an initiative for improvement; they will not prevent challenges! They are dynamic and fluid. You will reach the desired outcome of your plan and likely learn of new opportunities to enhance your program.

Assess

The self-assessments within Dr. Boyle's book, *Ensuring a Place at the Table,* may be used during the Assess stage. This is where the educational leader considers the WHY and acknowledges what is possible when we embrace the calling for inclusive practices in our Catholic schools. Using the self-assessments in Dr. Boyle's guidebook, the leader assesses needs, determines if this approach will "fit" in the school community, and considers the leadership, capacity, and organizational drivers that will promote the implementation of the initiative. These "implementation drivers" are depicted in the graphic, Implementation Drivers Tiangle. During the assess stage, the leader becomes aware of the competency drivers of Knowledge, Skills, and Dispositions within his/her school community.

In the Assess stage, gathering knowledge of where the community stands on inclusion as well as gathering data on students is important. The more a leader knows about the community as a whole, the more practical the Plan step will be. Dr. Boyle's self-assessments, the Knowledge/Skill/Disposition assessments from Chapter 3 of this book, and student data will inform the Plan.

IMPLEMENTATION DRIVERS TRIANGLE

IMPLEMENTATION DRIVERS
How we will shape an inclusive culture

Knowledge
- Rapport with mentors/coaches
- Comfort level with topic

Systems Intervention
- Diocesan and parish support
- Inclusion community drives change and continuous improvement process is identified within the Program Framework

Skills
- Belief in usefulness
- Direct intervention training
- Address topics identified in self-assessments

Facilitative Administration
- Support from administration, leads, department heads, etc.
- Can change organizational and system processes
- Modifications to admissions and hiring process put in place
- Present Level is known and target Level is established

Dispositions
- Consider dispositions
- Receptivity to training
- Is anyone exempt?

Data Driven Decisions
- Data from faculty and staff self-assessment is collected analyzed and considered
- Data from program framework is considered
- Data is reviewed to drive stakeholder decisions

Competency Drivers

Organizational Drivers

Leadership Drivers

Technical
- Time
- Funding

Adaptive
- Motivation of faculty and staff to change dispositions of stake holders
- Prepared to address conflict

Adopted from NIRN, 2019

Adopted from NIRN:https://nirn.fpg.unc.edu/learn-implementation/implementation-drivers

Plan

The second stage of implementation focuses on preparedness. The Plan is based upon the Self-Assessment data within Chapter 3 and Project Framework in Chapter 4. The leader is applying the data acquired from the self-assessments of faculty and staff knowledge, skills, and dispositions, and considering the factors which prepare a school community to provide inclusive educational practices as described in the project framework. This will determine the school level that best describes the educational community. Exploring the current reality establishes a baseline from which to build. There is no good or bad level, it just is what it is! The leader can best promote this initiative when sharing this data with the community. Is there a match between where we are, and the resources we need to reach the goal? If not, what information is needed to identify those resources?

We are glad you asked! Planning is multifaceted and also enables the school leader to learn more about the Knowledge, Skills, and Dispositions of faculty and staff. The sample scenarios in Chapter 3 may provide a place to start. Next, consider the Competency, Organizational, and Leaderships drivers depicted in the chart, the Implementation Drivers triangle. The components of each are included within the Program Framework. Knowledge of these drivers will support the plan and lessen the frustration of those who have implemented other programs that have ultimately gone by the wayside in the past. Your partners in this process must understand that successful implementation of any program requires two-four years. Build a community of others who feel the same way, create the "village" that will not permit this initiative to fail.

Execute

A well-developed plan to be executed will provide some peace of mind among the stakeholders. However, do not be discouraged if you must take a step back to plan and consider a variable that has changed or become available. Plan execution may begin with an overhaul of the professional development calendar in order to build capacity of faculty and staff, creation of a PLC, or welcoming parent and student ambassadors of inclusion. You have the capacity to meet the needs of students in your community, and you have achieved your initial goals for the program. This will take time and considerable efforts. The leader must ensure it is not dependent upon one individual, one program, or one student.

Refine

Full implementation of inclusive practices is worth the effort and a celebration of the outcomes your community has achieved. It is not a stopping point, rather just the beginning of continuous improvement. This plan can be embedded within accreditation processes, strategic planning for growth and stability, as well as plans to grow the school community. Refining your plan is necessary on an ongoing basis. Learn from missteps and successes, identifying what works well and not at all so that the plan meets the needs of the community at large. Consider how to meet the needs of a student with differences you have yet to serve, or a high school that is not prepared to continue the Catholic education you have provided during the K-8 years. Refinement requires assessment of practices on a consistent basis. Assessment may lead to changes in the plan, modifications to the execution of the plan, and provide opportunities for further refinement. The process is cyclical and dynamic.

TABLE 6

Program Development & Implementation Process

| 1 | Use self assessments to determine needs and dispositions of the community. Assess students to determine need. | 2 | Develop structures and put them in motion. | 3 | Be patient and consistent with the process to reach goals. Adjust as obstacles occur. |

Assess ➤ Plan ➤ Execute ➤ Refine

	Assess & Establish Why	• Catholic Mission	• Dignity of the Human Person
		• Catholic Social Teaching	• Church Documents
	Plan	Develop a plan. Be prepared to experience uncertainty and resistance due to:	
		• Lack of familiarity & training	• Need for growth in skills & knowledge
	Execute	• Support Structures	• Admissions Process
		• Training & Coaching	• Hire for Mission
		• Financial Plan	• Designate a Program Coordinator
	Refine	Success takes:	
		• Time • Faith	• Support • Cooperation
		• Patience • Persistence	• Consistency • Teamwork
	Goals	Level 1 ➤ Level 2 ➤ Level 3	

SPOTLIGHT ON ST. VALERIA SCHOOL

St. Valeria is an elementary school in the inner city with limited resources, a diverse population of ethnicities, poverty, and limited parent engagement. An energetic principal, fresh out of school, was hired by the pastor and began to ask questions such as "Why are students in third grade unable to read with proficiency?" and "Why are teachers leaving after only one - two years?" The faculty and staff were resigned to the notion that this was the reality of working in an inner city school without funding from a wealthy parish or alumni. They did the best they could with the previous leader who was satisfied with the status quo. No one asked "Why?" because they thought they already knew the answers.

At first this new principal was faced with criticism for asking the questions. Staff meetings and committee meetings focused on learning from the faculty, asking the questions with an open mind. The conversations frequently included questions that were data based, such as "How many first graders met the standards for promotion?", "What are the results of the annual achievement test?", and "Why are our fourth graders scoring so poorly on the annual achievement test?" They started talking about formative and summative data collected from homework, classwork, and tests. They found that although they collect a lot of data from assignment grades and testing, it was never utilized to make decisions. This was the principal's first objective; teach the faculty to understand the data they collect and make decisions for instruction based upon the data.

This was not easy, as many teachers felt intimidated by looking at data and describing what it meant. It casts shadows on students who were failing to meet benchmarks and brought about other questions that could not be easily answered. Training by the principal was not enough, so he reached out to his professional network to bring in others who could train the teachers. Using data became part of the conversation at all staff development opportunities. After two years, he felt that at least 70% of his teachers were comfortable with collecting and analyzing data. The next step was to teach them what to do with the data to increase student outcomes.

It was during this next step that the faculty realized the significant challenges that some students faced with learning. Because they understood the data, there were more conversations about how to help students who were not progressing. As the school's climate became more collaborative, there was less teacher turnover. Grade level meetings became time to learn about the struggles of specific students who were not responding to interventions such as small group instruction or one on one teaching before school in the morning. Teachers began to feel like they could make an impact in a student's achievement.

This step, during the third year of the principal's tenure, is when the faculty learned that students with disabilities were enrolled. This was not a sprint, but a marathon! The foundation had been built to recognize that St. Valeria was a Level 1 school. The principal learned about Dr. Michael Boyle's book, *Ensuring a Place at the Table*, and upon reading it he started to consider his school and the Knowledge, Skills, and Dispositions that he and others in the school possessed. Now that the faculty at St. Valeria has a greater understanding of data and has observed first hand that students with disabilities are on the campus, they are ready to begin the inclusive journey. Recruitment efforts are in place to add a resource teacher/specialist focused on inclusive practices. This person will work in concert with the principal as a framework is built to support all learners. The principal knows the questions to ask and the faculty and staff trust him to learn alongside them.

St. Valeria is still on this journey! They are committed to sharing their inclusive practices with their school community and building their capacity in the areas of Knowledge, Skills, and Dispositions.

Questions for Reflection

- How will I know my school community is ready to implement the plan?
- What resources do we currently have to support the drivers for competency? What resources will we need to build capacity?
- Are administrative policies in place to support the plan?
- How will I change the dispositions of faculty and staff?
- What technical changes can be made quickly?

CHAPTER 7:
FROM A DIOCESAN PERSPECTIVE

"In the case of many person with disabilities, integration into the Christian community may require nothing more than issuing an invitation and pursuing it. For some others, however, full participation can only come about if the Church exerts itself to devise innovative programs and techniques."

PASTORAL STATEMENT OF THE US CATHOLIC BISHOPS ON PERSONS WITH DISABILITIES, 1978

http://www.usccb.org/beliefs-and-teachings/what-we-believe/catholic-social-teaching/upload/Pastoral-Statement-of-U-S-Catholic-Bishops-on-Persons-with-Disabilities.pdf

Possibilities for Diocesan Level Leadership

Logically speaking, program development moves more quickly when there are fewer obstacles to progress. Most Catholic schools enjoy the benefit of independence due to subsidiarity, therefore allowing them to move through program development at a steady pace that is appropriate to the local community and without red tape. On the flip side, if a central office were trying to develop and implement programs in a top-down fashion, it would not move quickly or be the custom-fit program that each individual school may need.

So how can diocesan-level involvement help rather than hinder the process of inclusive program development for Catholic schools in a diocese or archdiocese? Here are some suggestions.

Big thinking and creativity on the part of diocesan educational leaders are needed to create guidance broad enough to be useful by all, or at least most, schools. Whether there are six schools or 206 schools to serve, general but effective principles and practices can be developed.

Here are some ideas.

Develop a team of professional practitioners that are willing to volunteer their services and expertise.

- Find individuals or organizations with areas of expertise that can be utilized by schools, such as speech and language pathologists, occupational therapists, retired special educators, psychologists, educational or child development experts at local universities, etc., etc. Partner with local organizations that serve visually impaired or hearing impaired individuals; partner with organizations that specialize in autism, fine motor development, early childhood social development, dyslexia, and other areas of specialization. Start by asking schools which local organizations they already work with to serve student needs outside of school.

    POSSIBILITIES: Having community volunteers available to be part of advisory boards or committees, as consultants, to coach teachers or troubleshoot specific cases opens up a world of possibility for schools with limited resources and personnel. Why try to manage volunteers from a diocesan level? Having a database of volunteers that leaders can call upon but also that schools can share can be more efficient than schools trying to manage their own league of experts.

    CHALLENGES: Initial organization of information will be one more task for the central office to manage. Vetting volunteers can also be challenging, so setting up a protocol BEFORE doing a call out to the community is important.
    Benefits outweigh the logistical drawbacks, and the value of the volunteers proves to be well worth the extra work.

Develop general guidance (or policies if it suits your arch/diocese) for schools that reinforces the mission of inclusive practices but also provides schools with clear protocols and resources.

- A guidebook, handbook, or set of policies around inclusive practices sets parameters and expectations. Schools need to understand that inclusion itself is not optional as stated in Canon law, but there is flexibility in how it looks from location to location. Each program will have its own nuances, strengths, and challenges based on the community and culture of the school.

    POSSIBILITIES: Clear expectations and the message that Catholic social teaching guides our mission to develop programs for exceptional learners must be provided from top educational and, preferably, arch/diocesan leaders. A common vision of purpose must be shared among all schools, and it must be set at the highest level.

CHALLENGES: If there is a guidebook or handbook rather than policies, there is more room for interpretation, which sometimes comes in the form of opting out. Policy has more grit than guidance, but policy development often takes many months to develop and circulate. Provide something early on. Guidebooks and handbooks for diversified learners in Catholic schools exist in several dioceses already, and some can be found through the NCEA resources to get you started. There is no need to reinvent the wheel.

Enlist direction and support from vicars and bishops.

- Nothing holds more value than the encouragement, wisdom, and guidance of your arch/diocesan shepherd. Ask your arch/bishop to write a letter or star in a video where he states his views on inclusive education. In some dioceses, there is a vicar that oversees education who might also be a good face for the support of the movement. Having this type of support impacts pastors as well.

Provide professional development at diocesan events or sponsor PD focused on inclusive practices.

- Providing PD at large-scale events can reach the masses and build momentum. Effective professional development excites educators and encourages conversation. Whether the topic of the training is implementing Universal Design for Learning, the dyslexic brain, or programs for including students with intellectual disabilities, there is so much to learn! If possible, plan mini-conference style events around the theme of inclusion and allow people to choose their topics. A general, unifying keynote followed by more specific topic breakouts is a tried and true format. When PD is provided by the arch/diocese, the message is clear that the topics offered are important to leadership.

  POSSIBILITIES: Getting people on the same page is important, and mass trainings get the ball rolling and provide the opportunity to get professionals together to begin conversations and make connections.

  CHALLENGES: Diocesan-led PD will likely be general in scope and may not meet the local needs. It will be important to encourage locations to discover the most pressing needs of the students and teachers at their locations and provide that specific PD onsite or in conjunction with other locations with similar needs.

Network with other diocesan educational leaders.

- The network of Catholic educational leaders across the country is strong. Personally, I have never called upon a colleague in another arch/diocese and been refused help. We share generously, we support one another, and we are deeply connected by the drive to build up Catholic education everywhere. Reach out and ask questions. Don't be afraid to ask to borrow job descriptions, handbooks, policies, or forms. Ask for recommendations for keynote speakers, trainers on specific topics, or online curriculum for intervention and enrichment. Knowing the successes and the struggles that are taking place in schools in other arch/dioceses can help guide important decisions and save lots of time!

Be the hub of the wheel.

- A person from the office of Catholic schools needs to be the hub. Gather schools' student support personnel for networking opportunities, and be sure all of the principals and student support professionals know who that person is. Ideally, eventually a PLC or online community may form that allows this group of people with similar roles to connect. However, until that happens, a person needs to be the hub!

  POSSIBILITIES: Provide opportunities for like-minded professionals in similar roles to support one another. As the connector, it is helpful for someone at the diocesan level to know the strengths of the folks in student support roles in the schools so he or she can help folks help each other. Host meetings of student support personnel at least a few times each year. Being part of the group allows the central office to have a finger on the pulse of which schools are building programs and which schools are not even coming to the table. Knowing which programs are good models to follow and who the leaders are is also important. A central connector from the office of Catholic schools can be a powerful symbol of the importance of exceptional learners to the arch/diocese as a whole. Schools should not feel like they are left to their own devices as they develop (or not develop!) exceptional learner programs. If student support professionals in the schools need guidance, they need to know who to contact in the central office.

  CHALLENGES: Early on, despite efforts to connect professionals with one another, the person in central office that acts as the hub will likely field many phone calls and emails that seems like they should be handled at the local level. Be patient, and keep in mind that the support of the central office will go a long way for schools who are uncertain about whether to begin a program, how to build a program, and who to ask for help! If there is NOT a designated Director of Programs for Diversified Learners (or other such title whose purpose is supporting these programs throughout the arch/diocese), the amount of time the designated hub spends on exceptional learner programs for a few years is going to be significant. Superintendents need to know that if a commitment to exceptional learner programs is expected at the school level, a similar commitment will need to be made at the arch/diocesan level. This means more responsibility for the person designated to be the hub—which may mean something else will have to give for that individual. The effectiveness of the support from the office of Catholic education by proxy of the bishop or archbishop will set the tone for progress at the school level.

Gather data and use it to understand the story of your arch/diocese.

- If you do not already do so, gather information on how many students in your schools have IEPs, have diagnosed learning disabilities, have student support plans, and/or receive services from LEAs. Track the number of students with diagnoses such as autism, ADHD, and dyslexia.

    POSSIBILITIES: Numbers can help guide PD options. Over time, they will also help you monitor information, find trends, clusters, and help diocesan leaders connect volunteer practitioners with schools that need their help. Having this information can also help a diocese compare apples-to-apples information with local districts, state, and national statistics. If there are grant opportunities for equipment, software, or training, these numbers will help support need and scope.

    CHALLENGES: Do not jump into data collection and analysis without presuppositions and with caution. Be prepared for a story you may not have expected from the data you collect. Imbalances and a lack of engagement from location to location may spark early frustration, but without the numbers, solving these problems cannot occur. Helping the people who complete data reports to know the difference, for example, between IEPs, METs, and student support plans may take some time. Understanding the difference between a learning disability and a diagnosis such as autism or ADHD may also take time. Accurate data will not come immediately; people need to learn the different categories and the language of special education. Be patient with the process.

At the risk of sounding obvious, the larger the number of schools in a given arch/diocese, the more challenging this process may be. Obstacles to building cohesion around a concept, even a deeply Catholic mission-driven concept, will exist. The reach of the office of Catholic schools and the personal relationships between central office leaders and school level personnel must be considered. If there is a disconnect between arch/diocesan level school leaders and local personnel, the challenge will be greater. Building programs for exceptional learners is, at its core, about relationships--parents and students connecting with teachers and school leaders; school leaders connecting with their teachers; school leaders and teachers connecting with central office leaders. Great ideas, even those focused on furthering the mission of the Church, will not develop fully without human connection at their core.

Questions for Reflection

- Is the arch/bishop of our arch/diocese supportive of inclusion initiatives? How do we know his position?
- Is the superintendent supportive of inclusion initiatives? How do we know?
- What support would we like the office of Catholic education to provide the schools to support inclusion initiatives?
- What data has the office of Catholic education gathered to show the existence of students with special needs in Catholic schools in our arch/diocese?
- What data would be helpful to see regarding students with special needs in our arch/diocese?

CHAPTER 8:

IN CLOSING...

The Lord makes firm the steps of the one who delights in him;
though he may stumble, he will not fall,
for the Lord upholds him with his hand.
PSALM 37:23-24

What Success Looks Like

Success can occur at any stage of program development. Whether a school is in pre-program development and just gathering data or in the transition from Level 2 to Level 3, success can and should be recognized and celebrated. Most important is beginning the journey to acknowledge and meet the needs of students' learning challenges. Once the community is on board to make the move, the table is set and ready.

Create a vision for your ideal Level 3. Dream big. What do you really need? Schools that have started from ground zero have achieved so much in a short time because the vision is strong, the need is apparent, and creative and responsible planning and budgeting can make so much happen. So, what is your ideal Level 3? Full-time counselor, speech and language pathologist, teachers with dual training in general ed and special ed, reading specialist, math interventionist, community volunteers with backgrounds in various specializations, strong partnerships with community organizations... Plan for your vision and stay the course.

The journey to developing a program for diversified learners may at times feel a bit like Mr. Toad's Wild Ride, perhaps a loop-de-loop at the carnival, maybe a walk through a dark room without a flashlight! Be ready for an experience that will be unique to the strengths and challenges of your community. Despite having checklists, how-to charts, plans, and the knowledge that you are doing God's good work, there is no guarantee that your road will be obstacle free or without detours. As any good roadtripper knows, though, the excitement is in the journey, and the detours are usually much more interesting than the planned itinerary. So be ready for and open to some twists and turns along the way. Building a strong team of supports and connecting with other educators with similar goals will make a significant difference when obstacles occur.

Success in early stages can take many forms:
- gathering data that tells a story to help leaders make a plan
- hiring on new people who are solid in Knowledge, Skills, and/or Dispositions for inclusive environments
- connecting with other leaders who are on the same journey
- watching teachers understand and use the data from universal screeners
- developing an admissions plan for students with IEPs or special needs
- creating a professional development plan that includes differentiated teaching and assessment
- successfully completing a CARE Team training (or first meeting!)
- trying an intervention never tried before and seeing it make a difference
- watching a struggling student feel proud of his or her accomplishment

Celebrate small and large wins expressing gratitude to those who contributed to them. Recognizing progress early on will build momentum to move your community toward the ideal Level 3 vision.

Rest assured that inclusion works for all students. Students who are gifted, or average learners, students who struggle, and students who have a disability will all grow in an inclusive setting. The SWIFT Education Center (national technical assistance center that builds school capacity for equity-based MTSS and inclusion) provides training and resources to public schools to build the capacity of school leaders and educators to support exceptional learners. The research they share provides a strong indication of the benefits of inclusive practices for the entire school community. The information we have shared here aligns with the SWIFT Center's premise that strong leadership, partnerships between the school and community, a system of supports derived from teacher knowledge and skills, and a framework to support inclusive education are the keys to successful implementation (SWIFT research support).

The SWIFT Center has compiled research funded by the Office of Special Education Programs that has been summarized below. This information is available for reproduction and is available on the Ideas That Work site.

Benefits of Inclusive Education for ALL Students:
Students without disabilities made significantly greater progress in reading and math when served in inclusive settings. (Cole, Waldron, Majd, 2004)

Students who provided peer supports for students with disabilities in general education classrooms demonstrated positive academic outcomes, such as increased academic achievement, assignment completion, and classroom participation. (Cushing & Kennedy, 1997)

Kalambouka, Farrell, and Dyson's (2007) meta-analysis of inclusive education research found 81% of the reported outcomes showed including students with disabilities resulted in either positive or neutral effects for students without disabilities.

Time spent engaged in the general education curriculum is strongly and positively correlated with math and reading achievement for students with disabilities. (Cole, Waldron, & Majd, 2004; Cosier, Causton-Theoharis, & Theoharis, 2013)

Students with intellectual disabilities who were fully included in general education classrooms made more progress in literacy skills compared to students served in special schools. (Dessemontet, Bless, & Morin, 2012)

Students with autism in inclusive settings scored significantly higher on academic achievement tests when compared to students with autism in self-contained settings. (Kurth & Mastergeorge, 2010).

Inclusive practices are research based and proven effective for all learners! We hope this will provide food for thought for even your toughest critic. The work cited above just scratch the surface. More research is being conducted to learn about inclusive practices in Catholic settings.

We hope you have enjoyed our stories and found the rubrics, frameworks, and self- assessments a support to your program. We welcome you to join us at Dr. Boyle's table where all have a seat, the settings are individualized, and the food is nourishment for the spirit!

QUESTIONS FOR REFLECTION

- Are we ready to create a vision? Has this process already begun?
- Who should be part of the visioning team? (Leaders, teachers, staff, parents, students, etc.?)
- What inspires me most to move forward? What will most inspire my school community to move forward?
- Of the information provided in this chapter, what is most surprising? Why?
- What are some action steps we can take to get started?

Appendix A

The Proportionate Share ratio is used to determine the proportion of the Local Education Agency's (LEA) total Part B subgrants under section 611(f) of the Act for Children aged 3 through 21, and under section 619(g) of the Act for Children aged 3 through 5, that is to be expended on services for parentally-placed private school children with disabilities enrolled in private elementary schools and secondary schools located in the LEA.

The following is an example of how the proportionate share is calculated:

There are 300 eligible children with disabilities enrolled in the Flintstone School District and 20 eligible parentally-placed private school children with disabilities enrolled in private elementary schools and secondary schools located in the LEA for a total of 320 eligible public and private school children with disabilities (note: proportionate share for parentally-placed private school children is based on total children eligible, not children served). The number of eligible parentally-placed private school children with disabilities (20) divided by the total number of eligible public and private school children with disabilities (320) indicates that 6.25 % of the LEA's subgrant must be spent for the group of eligible parentally-placed children with disabilities enrolled in private elementary schools and secondary schools located in the LEA. Flintstone School District receives $152,500 in federal flow through funds. Therefore, the LEA must spend $9,531.25 on special education or related services to the group of parentally-placed private school children with disabilities enrolled in private elementary schools and secondary schools located in the LEA. (Note: The LEA must calculate the proportionate share of IDEA funds before earmarking funds for any early intervening activities in §300.226).

The following outlines the calculations for the example of how the proportionate share is calculated.

Proportionate Share Calculation for Parentally-Placed Private School Children with Disabilities For Flintstone School District:	
Number of eligible children with disabilities in public schools in the LEA	300
Number of parentally-placed eligible children with disabilities in private elementary schools and secondary schools located in the LEA	20
Total number of eligible children	320
FEDERAL FLOW-THROUGH FUNDS TO FLINTSTONE SCHOOL DISTRICT	
Total allocation to Flintstone	$152,500
Calculating Proportionate Share:	
Total allocation to Flinstone	152,500
Divided by total number of eligible children	320
Average allocation per eligible child	476.5625
Multiplied by the number of parentally-placed children with disabilities	20
Amount to be expended for parentally-placed children with disabilities	$9,531.25

Appendix B to Part 300 - Proportionate Share Calculation. Retrieved from: https://sites.ed.gov/idea/regs/b/appendix-b

REFERENCES

Blase, K. A., Fixsen, D. L., Sims, B. J., & Ward, C. S. (2015). Implementation science: Changing hearts, minds, behavior, and systems to improve educational outcomes. Oakland, CA: The Wing Institute.

Boyle, M. (2018) Ensuring a Place at the Table: Serving Student with Disabilities in Catholic Schools. Arlington, VA: National Catholic Educational Association.

Cortiella, Candace and Horowitz, Sheldon H. The State of Learning Disabilities: Facts, Trends and Emerging Issues. New York: National Center for Learning Disabilities, 2014.

Fitzgibbons, M, Mahon, M, and Maus, A. (2008). The Care Team Approach: Problem-Solving Process for Change. Arlington, VA: National Catholic Educational Association.

Fixsen, D. L., Naoom, S. F., Blase, K. A., Friedman, R. M., & Wallace, F. (2005). Implementation research: A synthesis of the literature. (FMHI Publication No. 231). Tampa, FL: University of South Florida, Louis de la Parte Florida Mental Health Institute, National Implementation Research Network.

History of the IDEA. Retrieved from: https://www2.ed.gov/policy/speced/leg/idea/history.pdf

Mader, J. How Teacher Training Hinders Special Needs Students. The Atlantic. 1 Mar 2017. https://www.theatlantic.com/education/archive/2017/03/how-teacher-training-hinders-special-needs-students/518286/

The Individuals with Disabilities Education Act; Retrieved from: https://sites.ed.gov/idea/

National Center for Education Statistics. Retrieved from: https://nces.ed.gov/programs/coe/indicator_cgg.asp

SWIFT Education Center, Benefits of Inclusive Education for ALL Students. Retrieved from U.S. Department of Education, Institute of Education Sciences, National Center for Education Evaluation and Regional Assistance, What Works Clearinghouse.

ACKNOWLEDGEMENTS

Our deepest gratitude to all those who made this project possible.

Michael J. Boyle, Ph.D., Director, Andrew M. Greeley Center for Catholic Education at Loyola University Chicago for his contributions to educating students with disabilities in Catholic schools and inspiring this book through his publication Ensuring a Place at the Table.

Staff of the National Catholic Educational Association

Lisa Fischer, Ph.D., Founder of the Arizona Catholic Schools Disabilities Fund and the Exceptional Learners Advisory Board for the Diocese of Phoenix Catholic Schools

Sue Milano, Resource Program Coordinator, St. Francis Xavier Catholic School in Phoenix, Arizona

Jill Annable, Assistant Superintendent of Catholic Schools, Diocese of Grand Rapids

Linda Mosteller, Professional Development Specialist, formerly with the Arizona Department of Education

Amy M. Friel and Anna J. Friel for graphic design contributions

Grae Fischer for contributing original artwork for the book cover

Rachel Gatson, Assistant Principal, St. Gregory Catholic School in Phoenix, Arizona

Kathy Johnson, Reading Interventionist/Exceptional Learner Advisory Board Founding Member, Our Lady of Perpetual Help Catholic School in Scottsdale, Arizona

Mary Brownell, Exceptional Learner Advisory Board Member, Phoenix, Arizona

Joel, Lane and Quinlan Cejka for support and inspiration

Dave, Hannah, Georgia, and John Brooks for patience and love

ABOUT THE AUTHORS

Crystal Brooks is the director of inclusion at Notre Dame Preparatory in Scottsdale, Arizona. She has been working alongside special educators and administrators in public and Catholic schools for 15 years.

Colleen McCoy-Cejka is a product of 14 years of Catholic education in the Archdiocese of Chicago. She has been a Catholic school teacher in the Archdiocese of Indianapolis, a principal in the Diocese of Gary, and assistant superintendent in the Diocese of Phoenix.